THE
DIVINE
EXCHANGE

by

VICTORIA OLUBUNMI EDENIH

ISBN: 978-1-988439-30-3

DEDICATION

This book is humbly dedicated to him whom heaven and earth adore, even "Jesus Christ, who is the faithful witness, and the first begotten of the dead, and the prince of the kings of the earth. Unto him that loved us, and washed us from our sins in his own blood, And hath made us kings and priests unto God and his Father; to him be glory and dominion for ever and ever. Amen."
(Revelation 1:5).

CONTENTS

APPRECIATION

My gratitude goes to the Almighty God, our Maker, in whom we daily live, move and have our beings. In his greatness and majesty, he always calls things that are not as if they are. Who could have made a way on the Red Sea or caused water to come out of the rock? Who could have made Aaron's staff to bud and bear fruits overnight or filed up Rehab's and Ruth's names among the royals? Who could have made an axe head to float on water as a leaf, if not God? Our God changes times and seasons and does great wonders past finding out (Job 9:10). Thank you, Father of our Lord Jesus Christ, for you have made everything beautiful in your own time.

I want to appreciate my husband, Bro. Francis Oviomaigho Edenih, for his understanding and the helping hand he always lend whenever I am writing or tired. Some husbands will not help their wives and still hinder others from helping them for reasons best known to them, sir, not you. Thank you, Dad. I pray the Lord will stand by you always, cause his face to shine upon you and fulfill all your heart desires. You shall never be ashamed in Jesus mighty name.

My appreciation also goes to pastor Funke – Felix Adejumo, through whom my sleeping vision of writing books was awoken. I have never met her in person but had watched and listened to her on social media and had been blessed by God through her. When I heard her, I was motivated to pick up my abandoned project of writing. God bless you, ma. You have been elevated by God already; you shall never be brought low in Jesus mighty name.

I want to say a big thank you to my Pastor, Christ's Errand Boy, Pastor Nimibofa Samuel Victor, for his selfless lifestyle and commitment to making life meaningful for others. He knows nothing about hiding from others what might be profitable unto them; his love is amazing. I know what God had used you to do for me in the time past and now. Thank you, sir. The home for which you are daily sacrificing shall not slip out of your hands in Jesus mighty name.

My appreciation also goes to Pastor Segun Olugbemi, the General Overseer of Life's Way Assembly Worldwide, for his selfless guidance and support for the success of my writings. Despite the fact that we had not seen each other face to face; when your assistance was sought, you readily gave it more than we thought. Daddy, you surprised me! The Lord will be there for you always. You will not miss heaven in Jesus precious name.

I want to acknowledge the amazing support of Pastor Sola Oke. "Now he that ministereth seed to the sower both minister bread for your food, and multiply your seed sown, and increase the fruits of your righteousness" in Jesus glorious name. (2 Corinthians 9:10.)

I appreciate God on behalf of Pastor Daniel Idowu Olowe, The General Overseer of All Christians Evangelistic Ministry (a.k.a. The Last Days Revival Church) worldwide, for grooming me not through his messages only but also through personal examples of the sacrificial life of holiness. Dad, you will not labour in vain; the Lord is your reward in Jesus glorious name.

My appreciation also goes to the family of Pastor and mummy J. Edet, for their support in making the typing of the scripts very easy. The Lord's word says, "The liberal soul shall be made fat: and he that watereth shall be watered also himself." (Proverbs 11:25), so shall it be in your lives in Jesus' name. The Lord shall daily supply all your needs according to his riches in glory in Jesus' name.

It would have been impossible to take this book into fruition if not the sacrificial support and intervention of Mr. Gideon Aina. My brother, you have been there for me in a time like this, God will be there for you and your family always in Jesus' mighty name. You will never be put to shame in Jesus' name. Thank you very much.

I appreciate the labour of love and continuous mentoring of my father and mother in the Lord, Prof. Matthew S. and Mommy N. Abolarin. The heaven for which you have thus laboured will not slip from you in Jesus Christ' s name.

My appreciation also goes to my present district pastor and his wife, Prof. Ayoola and Mommy Iretiayo Olalusi. God bless you Dad and Mom for feeding me to satisfaction through his word.

I appreciate the moral support of Bro. (Engr.) Niyi Enibukun not only to me but also to my entire family. Sir, your humility is amazing! Thank you so much. God bless you.

My appreciation also goes to my aunt, a mother in Israel, Mrs. T. A. Aina for her contributions to make this book come to a limelight. Your light will never go into obscurity in Jesus Christ's name. Thank you, Mommy.

I must say a big thank you to my son in the Lord and his wife, Noble Daniel and Oyenike Alebiosu for their support and encouragement. God shall honour you in Jesus' mighty name.

I appreciate the moral support and some useful contributions of my daughter, Royal priesthood Ewomaoghene Oviomaigho. Thank you, love, may the Lord perfect all that concerns you in Jesus' mighty name.

I am equally grateful to God for granting me good understanding in his word through Apostle Paul of our time, for how would I have known if I had not been taught? The Lord had used his servant, Pastor W.F. Kumuyi, greatly to make the path of holiness and righteousness plain for all who cares to follow. In Proverbs chapter 31, verses 28 and 31 say: "Her children arise up, and call her blessed;" "Give her of the fruit of her hands; and let her own works praise her in the gates." I, therefore, joined the multitude of the saints all over the world to say a big thank you to my father in the Lord, Pastor W.F. Kumuyi, the General Superintendent of Deeper Christian Life Ministry worldwide for touching my life positively to be what God wants me to be. My Daddy, heaven shall be your reward in Jesus gracious name.

CHAPTER ONE

THE COSTLY EXCHANGE

Exchange is a deliberate act of giving out something and receiving something in return. In the primitive age, people directly exchange goods or services for other goods or services known as trade by barter. Nowadays, we exchange goods and services with money. Exchange happens daily in everyone's life. We daily replace or substitute one thing for another. We exchange money for domestic items or services such as airtime, barbing, plaiting, transportation, repairs and so on. However, the exchange I am talking about is ignorantly exchanging one's valuables for a less important, worthless or dangerous thing.

The first costly exchange that ever took place happened in the Garden of Eden when Eve ignorantly exchanged human's glory with the devil and got vanity, emptiness, nakedness, guilt, shame, curse and damnation in return. "**And the eyes of them both were opened, and they knew that they were naked; and they sewed fig leaves together, and made themselves aprons. And they heard the**

---

voice of the LORD God walking in the garden in the cool of the day: and Adam and his wife hid themselves from the presence of the LORD God amongst the trees of the garden. And the LORD God called unto Adam, and said unto him, Where art thou? And he said, I heard thy voice in the garden, and I was afraid, because I was naked; and I hid myself." (Genesis 3:7-10). Adam and Eve got the human race into slavery of sin as a result of the careless transaction that took place in that garden with the devil and got the nature of sin and death in return. "For as in Adam all die..." (I Corinthians 15:22). God's word said the reward of the dialogue and the eaten of the forbidden fruit that happened in Genesis chapter 3: 1-6 is death. "And unto Adam he said, Because thou hast hearkened unto the voice of thy wife, and hast eaten of the tree, of which I commanded thee, saying, Thou shalt not eat of it: cursed is the ground for thy sake; in sorrow shalt thou eat of it all the days of thy life; Thorns also and thistles shalt it bring forth to thee; and thou shalt eat the herb of the field; In the sweat of thy face shalt thou eat bread, till thou return unto the ground; for out of it wast thou taken: for dust thou art, and unto dust shalt thou return." (Genesis 3:17-19).

The costly exchange that took place in the Garden of Eden needed a costlier, divine exchange to buy back humanity from the slavery of sin and eternal doom. **"And I will put enmity between thee and the woman, and between thy seed and her seed; it shall bruise thy head, and thou shalt bruise his heel;"** (Genesis 3:15). **"Wherefore, as by one man sin entered into the world, and death by sin; and so death passed upon all men, for that all have sinned:"** (Romans 5:12). **"But not as the offence, so also is the free gift. For if through the offence of one many be dead, much more the grace, which is by one man, Jesus Christ, hath abounded unto many."** (Romans 5:15). The costlier and divine exchange that could solve the human problem of sin and its consequence must involve stainless, guiltless blood of a human, to which only Christ Jesus was found qualified. **".. and without the shedding of blood is no remission."** **"So Christ was once offered to bear the sins of many; and unto them that look for him shall he appear the second time without sin unto salvation."**(Hebrews 9:22b; 28). The captor left the woman alone after the fall. He thought the yoke of slavery imposed on human was permanent; how wrong he was! In his love, God, who is higher than the captor, gave the world his only begotten Son, who willfully laid down his life to redeem humanity from the dominion of the captor. Redemption from eternal slavery would not have been possible without the shedding of blood. Known unto God are all his works from the beginning of the world. In his wisdom and mercy, he provided for the redemption of the helpless. Praise the Lord! The solution was pure and perfect, for God himself provided it through his only begotten Son, Jesus Christ, the righteous one. The solution was potent because the Creator of heaven and earth alone who provided the solution has power over the captor. Since Christ's sacrifice was potent and is still potent and suffices all through eternity, there is no other solution acceptable unto God. **"Neither is there salvation in any other: for there is none other name under heaven given among men, whereby we must be saved."** (Acts 4:12) Christ Jesus was wounded for our transgressions and bruised for our iniquities according to God's own design. The chastisement of our peace was upon him and with his stripes, we are healed (Isaiah 53:5). Christ's sacrifice got us total freedom from sin and eternal destruction in hell. It provided for our peace in this troublous world and also for our healing.

The devil tactically led humanity astray from the favour of the creator. He was once in heaven but forfeited it through sin.

"How art thou fallen from heaven, O Lucifer, son of the morning! how art thou cut down to the ground, which didst weaken the nations! For thou hast said in thine heart, I will ascent into heaven, I will exalt my throne above the stars of God; I will sit also upon the mount of the congregation, in the sides of the north: I will ascend above the heights of the clouds; I will be like the most High." (Isaiah 14:12-14). "Thou hast been in Eden the garden of God; every percous stone was thy covering, the sardius, topaz, and the diamond, the beryl, the nohx, and the jasper, the sapphire, the emerald, and the carbuncle, and gold; the workmanship of thy tabrets and of thy pipes was prepared in thee in the day that thou wast created. Thou art the anointed cherub that covereth; and I have set thee so: thou wast upon the holy mountain of God; thou hast walked up and down in the midst of the stones of fire. Thou wast perfect in thy ways from the day that thou wast created, till iniquity was found in thee. By the multitude of thy merchandise they have filled the midst of thee with violence, and thou hast sinned: therefore I will cast thee as profane out of the mountain of God: and I will destroy thee, O covering cherub, from the midst of the stones of fire. Thine heart was lifted up because of thy beauty; thou hast corrupted thy wisdom by reason of thy brightness: I will cast thee to the ground, I will lay thee before kings, that they may behold thee." (Ezekiel 28:13-17). No one tempted the devil, who was called Lucifer, to sin but himself and so he was cast down to the earth. He, in his great wrath, would not want anyone, not even those who are serving him, to make the heaven he had lost. He daily moves about like a roaring lion seeking whom he will destroy. In his craftiness, he led man to eternal separation from God. Christ, the sinless Son of God, came in the flesh and bore the penalty for the sin he never committed. "For Christ also hath once suffered for sins, the just for the unjust, that he might bring us to God, being put to death in the flesh, but quickened by the Spirit..." (I Peter 3:18).

We have seen how the enemy came in a friendly and concerned manner to steal our liberty and gave us a heavy yoke of affliction and oppression. He deadened man's conscience against godliness; man would rather walk in accordance with the trends of this world rather than pleasing the Lord. The power of the enemy, who seemed to have gotten the glory, controls every activity of man to always walk contrary to the will of God. It is easy for man to always rebel against the Lord, for rebellion is already in the blood. **"Wherein in time past ye walked according to the course of this** world, according to the prince of the power of the air, the spirit that now worketh in the children of disobedience: Among whom also we all had our conversation in times past in the lusts of our flesh and of the mind; and were by nature the children of wrath, even as others." (Ephesians 2:2-3). No none needs to teach another to commit sin; everyone knows how because it is in the blood. A baby that can neither talk nor walk and still sucking knows when he or she is wrong. A child that is sucking that wants to hurt will carefully press his gums on you, remove his mouth and watch your reaction. If you do nothing to correct that child but smile, he will press a little harder. If you only smile and do not correct the child, he will press the hardest. Who taught the baby that mum can feel pain if you do that? Who taught the child to check the mother's face to know whether she feels pain or not? A baby of about six or seven months old was always sucking and would not want to eat any other food after the exclusive period. The mother rebuked her by saying. "you only like to suck but do not like to eat any other food." That child removed her mouth and cried. That child refused to suck again and did not eat another food given to her. The boss of her mother noticed the change in the baby's attitude since the mother talked that way. She gently carried the child from her mother, begged and called her pet names and told the mother to give her suck to know whether what happened was just a coincidence. The mother also begged the child, called her pet names and gave her suck. To the bewilderment of both women, the baby sucked. Who taught a baby to know when he is hurting and when he is hurt? The mother repeated the action in another place; the baby also repeated the same action; by that time she was nine months old. An elderly father was with them, took the baby and held her to himself, begged and called her pet names and told the mother to give her suck. The baby looked at the mother with mixed feelings, the mother begged her and she sucked. That was the last time the mother would behave that way. Please, who taught babies how to express displeasure when they are hurt? When you feed them and they are satisfied, they look at your face and smile as if saying thank you but when you say or do something they are not comfortable with, though you did not beat them, they cry and even refuse food – what is that if not sin? The sinful nature was born with them. They know how to sin as soon as they are born without anybody teaching them. "**The wicked are enstranged from the womb: they go astray as soon as they be born, speaking lies.**" (Psalms 58:3). "**For all have sinned, and come short of the glory of God;**" (Romans 3; 23). All, including children, have sinned. The condition of man after the fall was so terrible that God had to intervene immediately. Today, Calvary has made a sure way of total freedom over Satan, the captor of man; sin, the cause of separation from God and hell, the consequence of sin. You can be free from that evil, inherent nature of sin if you want to. The grace of God has made salvation free for all and sundry. Salvation is too costly that not even the richest of humanity can afford it; hence it is made free for all by the Creator. **"But God who is rich in mercy, for his great love wherewith he loved us, Even when we were dead in sins, hath quickened us together with Christ, (by grace ye are saved;)"** (Ephesians 2:4-5). You are included in God's plan of salvation, you might not have known this but it is true for God's word said so. **"But God who is rich in mercy, for his great love wherewith he loved us, Even when we were dead in sins, hath quickened us together with Christ, (by grace ye are saved;)"** (Ephesians 2:4-5). No matter the level of sin you have committed, you can be free, for Christ had made provision for your freedom. The question is, **Do you want to be made free?** You are not just a sinner because of the things you are doing wrong; you are sinning because of the in-built sinful nature in you. Christ Jesus is divinely chosen and exalted to take away the sins of the whole world. **"The next day John seeth Jesus coming unto** him, and saith, Behold the Lamb of God, which taketh away the sin of the world." (John 1:29). You need not involve yourself in any other sacrifice than coming to Christ, who has borne the chastisement for your sins in true repentance and then he will forgive and save you. Only Jesus Christ can save. "This Jesus hath God raised up, whereof we all are witnesses." (Acts 2:32). "Neither is there salvation in any other: for there is none other name under heaven given among men, whereby we must be saved." (Acts 4:12). ".. Believe on the Lord Jesus Christ, and thou shalt be saved, and thy house." (Acts 16:31). The load of sin and its consequence you daily bear is too much for you. Do you know that God is angry with every sinner who cares less about his or her salvation daily? You hear much about hell but you care less about escaping it. You hear much about eternity; you care less about preparing for it. Where are the godless mightiest of ages past? Where are the scorners of ages past? Where are the ferocious persecutors of the early church now? Were they able to gain the entire world and retain it? (Mark 8:36). The day the owner of their lives withheld their breath, they could not resist him, they returned to the earth; in that very day, their thoughts perished. (Psalms 146:4). Certainly, there is time for everything; the time we were born and the time we would die. Whether literate or illiterate, we will die one day. We shall all be judged based on things we have done while in the flesh. **"For we must all appear before the judgment seat of Christ; that every one may receive the things done in his body, according to that he hath done, whether it be good or bad."** (2 Corinthians 5:10). No human will be justified before God without salvation through Christ, for all our righteousness are as filthy rags to God; hence you really need justification through Christ now before your death to guarantee you heaven when you die. If you die without salvation, you will be lost forever in hell. The Lord is saying repent and turn unto me, for why will you perish? **"Cast away from you all your transgressions, whereby ye have transgressed; and make you a new heart and a new spirit; for why will ye die, O house of Israel? For I have no pleasure in the death of him that dieth, saith the Lord GOD: wherefore turn yourselves, and live ye."** (Ezekiel 18:31-32). Believe in your heart the sacrifice Christ made for you on the cross, repent of your sins, confess and forsake them. Invite Christ Jesus into your heart by faith. Have a change of attitude by feeding daily on God's word and living by it. By so doing, divine exchange will happen on your behalf and your own name will be written in God's book of life. It is mandatory for you to be born again if you must inherit the kingdom of God. **"Jesus answered and said unto** him, verily, verily, I say unto thee, Except a man be born again, he cannot see the kingdom of God." "Marvel not that I said unto thee, Ye must be born again." (John 3:3, 7). Till eternity Christ remains the only solution to every problem or bondage of man. He will hear you when you call on him in righteousness. Let righteousness cloth you like a garment daily. Right everything you have done wrong and be at peace with everybody no matter what he has or has not done to you. "Follow peace with all men, and holiness, without which no man shall see the Lord:" (Hebrews 12"14). Make up your mind to follow Jesus whether in wealth or in want."If any man will come after me, let him deny himself, and take up his cross daily, and follow me." (Luke 9:23).

However, if you read this book and yet remain unsaved, in eternity, you will remember this message and how you scorned it. In agony, you will cry bitterly but there will be no one to ease your pain or comfort you. "And the devil that deceived them was cast into the lake of fire and brimstone, where the best and the false prophet are, and shall be tormented day and night for ever and ever. And I saw a great white throne, and him that sat on it, from whose face the earth and the heaven fled away; and there was found no place for them. And I saw the dead, small and great, stand before God; and the books were opened: and another book was opened, which is the book of life: and the dead were judged out of those things which were written in the books, according to their works. And the sea gave up the dead which were in it; and death and hell delivered up the dead which were in them: and they were judged every man according to their works. And death and hell were cast into the lake of fire. This is the second death. And whosoever was not found written in the book of life was cast into the lake of fire." (Revelation 20:10-15).

IF I GAINED THE WORLD (ANNA OLANDER)

(1)   If I gained the world, but lost the Saviour, We're my life worth living for a day? Could my yearning heart find rest and comfort In the things that soon must past away? If I gained the world, but lost the Saviour, Would my gain be worth the life long strife? Are all earthly pleasures worth comparing For a moment with a Christ filled life?

(2)   Had I wealth and love in fullest measure, And a name revered both far and near, Yet no hope beyond, no harbour waiting, Where my stormtossed vessel I could steer; If I gained the

world, but lost the Saviour, Who endured the cross and died for me, Could then all the world afford a refuge, Wither, in my anguish I might flee?

(3) O what emptiness ! Without the Saviour 'Mid the sins and sorrows here below! And eternity, how dark without Him! Only night and tears and endless woe! What tho' I might live without the Saviour, When I come to die, how would it be? O to face the valley's gloom without Him! And without Him all eternity!

(4) O the joy of having all in Jesus! What a balm the broken heart to heal! Ne'er a sin so great, but He'll forgive it, Nor a sorrow that He does not feel! If I have but Jesus, only Jesus, Nothing else in all the world beside__ O then ev'rything is mine in Jesus; For my needs and more He will provide.

AT CALVARY (William R. Newell)

(1) Years I spent in vanity and pride,
Caring not my Lord was crucified,
Knowing not it was for me He died,
On Calvary.

Mercy there was great, and grace was free;
Pardon there was multiplied to me;
There my burdened soul found liberty,
At Calvary.

(2) By God's Word at last my sin I learned;
Then I trembled at the law I'd spurned;
Till my guilty soul imploring turned,
To Calvary.

(3) Now I've given to Jesus everything,
Now I gladly own Him as my King;
Now my raptured soul can only sing,
Of Calvary.

(4) Oh! The love that drew salvation's plan!
Oh! The grace that brought it down to man!

Oh! The mighty gulf that God did span,

At Calvary.

HE DIED OF A BROKEN HEART
(THOMAS DENNIS)

(1) Have you read the sto-ry of the Cross, where Je-sus bled and died;

Where your debt was paid by His precious blood that flowed from His wounded side?

Chorus:

He died of a bro-ken heart for you; He died of a bro-ken heart;

Up-on a tree, for you, for me, He died of a bro-ken heart.

(2) Have you read how they placed the crown of thorns, Up-on His brow for you, When He prayed, "For-give them, oh, for-give; They know not what they do?"

(3)   Have you read how He saved the dy-ing thief, When hanging on the tree, When he looked with plead-ing eyes and said, "Dear Lord, re-mem-ber Me?"

(4)   Have you read that He looked to heaven and said, "Tis finished?" "Twas for thee! Have you ev-er said, "I thank Thee, Lord, For giv-ing Thy life for me?"

I WANT TO SEE JESUS, DON'T YOU?
(ADA JANE BLENKHORN)

(1)   There is One loved me so, that for me he died; He's my dear, precious Saviour so true; On the cross for my sins, He was crucified; I want to see Jesus, don't you?

I want to see Jesus, don't you? My Saviour so faithful and true;... When I reach the strand, of that love-bright land, O I want to see Jesus, don't you?...

(2)   When I'm weary and faith He is always near, With his joy He my strength doth renew; And He comforts my heart, speaking words of cheer: I want to see Jesus, don't you?

(3)   Holy angels keep watch, o'er me thro' the night, And each morning He guards me anew; In the smile of His love, doth my soul delight; I want to see Jesus, don't you?

(4)   He is fairer than lily or rose to me, And His blessings fall soft as the dew; O my heart, how it longs, His dear face to see: I want to see Jesus, don't you?

(5)   There's a place for my soul, that He doth prepare; And its beauty by faith I can view; First of all, when I enter that mansion fair, I want to see Jesus, don't you?

CHAPTER TWO

CARELESS EXCHANGE

arelessness, as the name sounds, is not caring or worrying about the aftermath of an action. So many people do not really care about the repercussion of their actions or inactions. If other people are ignorant of the devil's devices, believers in Christ should not, for we are warned by the Lord thus: **"Watch and pray, that ye enter not into temptation..."** (Matthew 26:41). Also, in 1 Peter 5:8, we are warned: **"Be sober, be vigilant; because your adversary the devil, as a roaring lion, walketh about, seeking whom he may devour: whom resist steadfast in the faith, knowing that the same afflictions are accomplished in your brethren that are in the world."** Our adversary is not resting at all. Despite the defeat in Eden, he is not ready to give up on anybody, whether saved or unsaved. The weapon of temptation remains what he uses often. He tempted Eve with food and fell man. He tempted Christ with the same food but failed. He tempted some mighty men with women and fell them while others remained unconquerable and would not be defiled by women. For others, he deceived them with riches. They are very careless with their souls; they would rather have riches at the expense of their souls. Believers are not to be ignorant of the devices of the devil.

Our faith is very precious; we must jealously keep it till the Lord comes. It may seem insignificant to you, what you do not really value, there is someone that is eyeing it. We must not be careless like Esau with our salvation. Although salvation is free, it is never cheap because it costs the Saviour his life. Salvation is our birthright. That sanctification we have received must be kept jealously no matter the pressure. Esau exchanged his birthright with a plate of food. "**And Jacob sod pottage: and Esau came from the field, and he was faint: And Esau said to Jacob, Feed me, I pray thee, with that same red pottage; for I am faint: therefore was his name called Edom. And Jacob said, Sell me this day thy birthright. And Esau said, Behold, I am at the point to die: and what profit shall this birthright do to me? And Jacob said, Swear to me this day; and he sware unto him: and he sold his birthright unto Jacob. Then Jacob gave Esau bread and pottage of lentils; and he did eat and drink, and rose up, and went his way; thus Esau despised his birthright.**" (Genesis 25:29-34) Worldly gain is like a plate of food compared to heaven's treasure. Believers would be of all men most miserable if we gain the world but forfeit eternal bliss. We must value our relationship with Christ more than certificates or any other worldly accomplishment. Esau should have endured the hunger and cooked his own food to keep his birthright. He could as well drunk water to keep his spirit and soul together and find something to cook. Hunger revealed the true nature of Esau. He had never been serious with the issue of his birthright. He valued his stomach more than any birthright. He surely lacked self-control over his appetite and could sacrifice anything to fill his stomach. His stomach was his true god. When he was told to swear and sell his birthright, he readily did so; what a pity! Esau carelessly exchanged his birthright for a meal; this is disheartening! As a lady, when you were told to give your body and get a lucrative job or pass an exam, what was your reaction? Did you yield to that temptation? As a man, when you were told to give a bribe before you can pass your exams or get a job for yourself or a school for your child, did you yield? Some would even renounce the Lord, the Judge of the universe, to keep their jobs. One thing is sure; everything that has a beginning has an end. Your suffering on earth has a beginning; it surely has an end. Why then will you, because of the present light affliction and compromise your faith? Why do you want to sacrifice your endless glorious future on the altar of instant fleshly gratification? You must continue in serving God in holiness and righteousness all your days. Soon he that shall come will come and not tarry (Hebrews 10:37).

Esau was likened to an immoral and a profane person because of his nonchalant attitude to his glorious inheritance. "**Lest there be any fornicator, or profane person, as Esau, who for one morsel of meat sold his birthright.**" (Hebrews 12:16). How careful and watchful are you over your life? Good things of life are good. We are not exempted from getting earthly blessings. We can always get our portions of the goodies on earth by asking our Father, who truly controls both heaven and earth. The Psalmist said, "**I will lift up mine eyes unto the hills, from whence cometh my help. My help cometh from the LORD, which made heaven and earth.**" Every believer must be careful not to exchange his or her glory for shame and regret because of lack or suffering. That lack or suffering came, not to stay but to pass away; very soon, you shall laugh at every storm if you faint not. Do not be smarter than God in your decisions by applying worldly wisdom in getting riches, marriage partner, and certificates and so on. Rest on God for all your needs for our sufficiency is of him. (2 Corinthians 3:5).

There is hope for every profane Esau that would come to Christ, for whosoever shall call on the name of the Lord shall be saved. Christ is the way to recover everything you have lost. He is the way to gaining eternal haven of rest. Desist from trading with your never-dying soul. Do not wait too late like Esau before seeking restoration of your lost birthright. If you scorn this message because of unbelief and keep dining with Lucifer because of worldly wealth till death visits you, you will not only go naked as you came but miss eternal life in heaven. You truly need Jesus for a total recovery of your losses. Now is the acceptable time, now is the day of your salvation. **"(For he saith, I have heard thee in a time accepted, and in the day of salvation have I succoured thee: behold, now is the accepted time; behold, now is the day of salvation.)"** (2 Corinthians 6:2). **"For whosoever shall call upon the name of the Lord shall be saved."** (Romans 10:13).

SPRINGS OF THE LIVING WATER
(JOHN W. PETERSON)

(1) I thirsted in the barren land of sin and shame,

And nothing satisfying there I found,

But to the blessed cross of Christ one day I came,

Where springs of living water did abound.

Chorus:

Drinking at the springs of living water,

Happy now am I my soul they satisfy,

Drinking at the springs of living water,

O wonderful and bountiful supply.

(2) How sweet the living water from the hills of God,

It makes me glad and happy all the day,

Now glory grace and blessing mark the path I've trod,

I'm shouting hallelujah every day.

(3) O sinner won't you come today to Calvary,

A fountain there is flowing deep and wide,

The Saviour now invites you to the water free,

Where thirsting spirits can be satisfied.

COME OVER

(1)   There's a land of peace and plenty, and its gates are open wide,

And the pure in heart and holy, in its shelter may abide;

It is not thro' gates of glory that a soul must enter in;

But all who would find entrance there must leave the ways of sin;

Chorus:

Come over, come over, to the land of corn and wine,

There is nothing can compare with the many holy pleasures there,

Come over, come over, leave the desert plain below,

And come away, away, come over.

(2)   There is bread of heaven growing, in its fair and fertile fields,

And the wine of love its vineyard to the thirsting mortal yields;

There are mountain heights of glory that await the trav'lers rod,

And blest retreats where empty souls draw nearer unto God;

(3)   Who would stay without its borders, in the desert hard and drear, when the luscious grapes of Eschol are so very, very near?

Enter in then with rejoicing, for the Lord is on your side,

And in His glorious presence evermore you shall abide.

CHAPTER THREE

THE DIVINE EXCHANGE

"The heart is deceitful above all things, and desperately wicked: who can know it?" (Jeremiah 17:9). "And we know that we are of God and the whole world lieth in wickedness." (I John 5:19). "For wickedness burneth as the fire..." (Isaiah 9:18).

The whole world, including where you are, lies in wickedness. Many in our world do not have the fear of God. "There is no fear of God before their eyes." (Romans 3:18). "Because sentence against an evil work is not executed speedily; therefore the heart of men is fully set in them to do evil." (Ecclesiastes 8:11). It is only God that can deliver an innocent from every snare of the wicked. Whenever I read the story of Ahab's subtle instruction to Jehoshaphat to remain in royal apparel, I am always surprised. Jehoshaphat was an Israelite as Ahab. They were both kings. Jehoshaphat was Ahab's in-law because his son had married Ahab's daughter. "Now Jehoshaphat had riches and honour in abundance, and joined affinity with Ahab." (2

Chronicles 18:1). "**And he walked in the way of the kings of Israel, as did the house of Ahab: for the daughter of Ahab was his wife: and he did evil in the sight of the LORD.**" (2 Kings 8:18). One would have expected strong cord of sincere love between Ahab and Jehoshaphat, but the depravity in Ahab's life would not allow it. Only God knows the heart of man; hence, he warned: "**Trust ye not in a neighbour, put ye not confidence in a friend; keep the doors of thy mouth from her that lieth in thy bosom.**"(Micha 7:5). Jehoshaphat joined affinity with Ahab. He allowed and supported his son's marriage to Ahab's daughter, yet Ahab wisely switched over his death penalty on Jehoshaphat. If not for divine intervention, Jehoshaphat would have died that day. The heart is truly deceitful above all things and desperately wicked. God frowned against putting our trust in flesh. "**Thus saith the LORD Cursed be the man that trusteth in man, and maketh flesh his arm, and whose heart departeth from the LORD. For he shall be like the health in the desert... Blessed is the man that trusteth in the LORD, and whose hope the LORD is.**" (Jeremiah 17:5-7). There are those who solely put their trust in their business. If the business folds up, they faint or die. There are others that put their hope on relations or friends; should any of these people fail, their lives will be shattered.

Jehoshaphat requested the king to let them seek the help of God, which they did but king Ahab hated the genuine prophet of God and his message with perfect hatred. Instead of humbling himself before the Almighty God and retreated, he commanded his servants to feed Micaiah, the man who told him the mind of God with bread and water of affliction till he returned from the battle; God did not permit him to return safely. **"And the king of Israel said, Take Micaiah, and carry him back unto Amon the governor of the city, and to Joash the king's son; And say, Thus saith the king, Put this fellow in the prison, and feed him with bread of affliction and with water of affliction, until I come in peace. And Micaiah said, if thou return at all in peace, the LORD hath not spoken by me. And he said, Hearken, O people, every one of you"** (I Kings 22:26-28). Did he return from that journey? **"And a certain man drew a bow at a venture, and smote the king of Israel between the joints of the harness: wherefore he said unto the driver of his chariot, Turn thine hand, and carry me out of the host; for I am wounded. And the battle increased that day: and the king was stayed up in his chariot against the Syrians, and died at even: and the blood ran out of the wound into the midst of the chariot."** (1 Kings 22:34-35). Ahab never returned from that journey. He was warned not to go but he was too great to be controlled by his Maker. He knew God was angry with him every day because of his wickedness and idolatry, yet he was too big to repent before God in whose hand was his soul. He had military prowess and full of idolatry. He was wrathful to the man that loved him so much to have told him the truth so he would avoid that death. He ignored God's instruction and treated the man of God with disdain. He was under God's wrath yet was harassing the man of God with malicious words. Some people are like Ahab; they hate the truth but delight in lies and flatteries. They hate correction but like deception. God is angry with them daily because of the yoke of sin they refuse to drop at the cross yet they feast often. God's word said, "**A prudent man forseeth the evil, and hideth himself: but the simple pass on, and are punished. By humility and the fear of the LORD are riches, and honour, and life.**" (Proverbs 22:3-4). What is the essence of your rejoicing when with all your getting, you lack salvation? You have power like Ahab; you can do and undo, yet you lack salvation; you are very poor and wretched.

Ahab knew God's word would definitely come to pass; he then wisely advised Jehoshaphat to remain in the royal robe and that he would dress like one of the soldiers and go into the battle but Jehoshaphat should be on the throne. That man was a good planner but he was not as wise as God, who made him and gave him his wisdom and that was against him because of his vileness and refusal to change. No one can fight against his Maker and succeed. Are you a sinner? Do not harden your heart against the Lord like Ahab. Where is Ahab now? The Lord removed him from the face of the earth in his anger; can he be with God in heaven now? That man died in his transgression and we all know that without holiness, no man can see the Lord. The earlier you humble yourself before God in true repentance, the better for you. You have a lot to gain from the Lord if you let him cleanse your sins and rule your heart. Ahab continued in his subtle planning and wisely switched over his death penalty on Jehoshaphat but there is God in heaven who ruled in the affairs of man.".. that the living may know that the most High ruleth in the kingdom of men…" (Daniel 4:17). "**The Lord knoweth how to deliver the godly out of temptations, and to reserve the unjust unto the day of judgment to be punished:**" (2 Peter 2:9). The Lord delivered Jehoshaphat when he cried out. "**And the Lord shall deliver us from every evil work, and will preserve us unto his heavenly kingdom; to whom be glory for ever and ever. Amen.**" (2 Timothy 4:18). Jehoshaphat did not waste any time at all, he cried out and the Lord helped him. The Psalmist said, "**I will call upon** the LORD, who is worthy to be praised, so shall I be saved from my enemies." Also, "This poor man cried, and the Lord heard him, and saved him out of all his troubles." The Almighty caused a divine exchange, a divine switch-over, Jehoshaphat was rescued and Ahab died his death. There will be a divine exchange on your behalf as a child of God. God's word assured us that whosoever digs a pit shall fall there in. " Whoso diggeth a pit shall fall therein: and he that rolleth a stone, it will return upon him." (Proverbs 26:27). If you are a sheep in Christ's fold, the Lord will deliver you from every evil work and preserve you to his heavenly kingdom in Jesus' name.

The Jews were roped by Haman because of one man's attitude and would have been exterminated if not for God's intervention. "After These things did king Ahasuerus promote Haman the son of Hammedatha the Agagite, and advanced him, and set his seat above all the princes that were with him. And all the king's servants, that were in the king's gate, bowed, and referenced Haman: for the king has so commanded concerning him. But Mordecai bowed not, nor did him reverence. And when Haman saw that Mordecai bowed not, nor did him reverence, then was Haman full of wrath. And he thought scorn to lay hands on Mordecai alone; for they had shewed him the people of Mordecai: wherefore Haman sought to destroy all the Jews that were throughout the whole kingdom of Ahasuerus, even the people of Mordecai. And Haman said unto king Ahasuerus, There is a certain people scattered abroad and dispersed among the people in all the province of thy kingdom; and their laws are diverse from all people; neither keep they the king's laws: therefore it is not for the king's profit to suffer them. If it please the king, let it be written that they may be destroyed: and I will pay ten thousand talents of silver to the hands of those that have the charge of the business, to bring it into the king's treasuries. And the king took his ring from his hand, and gave it unto Haman the son of Hammedatha the Agagite, the Jew's enemy. And the king said unto Haman, The silver is given unto thee, the people also, to do with them as it seemeth good to thee." (Esther 3:1-2; 5-6; 8-11). This was the horrible and hopeless situation the Jew's found themselves at that time. The doom of the whole race was determined by one man, Haman and sealed by the king whose writing could none reverse. ".. for the writing which is written in the king's name, and sealed with the king's ring, may no man reverse." (Esther 8:8). However, the Jews remembered their God and called upon him. The Lord heard and delivered them, he will hear your cry and deliver you.

"Then Esther bade them return Mordecai this answer, Go, gather together all the Jews that are present in Shushan, and fast ye for me, and neither eat nor drink three days, night or day: I also and my maidens will fast likewise; and so will I go in unto the king, which is not according to the law: and if I perish, I perish. So Mordecai went his way, and did according to all that Esther had commanded him." (Esther 4:15-17).These people called upon the Lord in their affliction and He heard and delivered them. Your case cannot be different, God will deliver you. He delivered Mordecai and the Jews from Haman; Haman was hung on the gallows he made for Mordecai. " So they hanged Haman on the gallows that he had prepared for Mordecai. Then was the king's wrath pacified." (Esther 7:10). Serve the Lord in righteousness for purity is power. Purity attracts you to God and makes His ears attentive to your cry. We are told "God heareth not sinners: but if any man be a worshipper of God, and doeth his will, him he heareth." (John 9: 31). There is no situation so bad that God cannot change for good. He is the Lord that changes times and seasons. " And he changeth the times and seasons: he removeth kings, and setteth up kings: he giveth wisdom unto the wise, and knowledge to them that know understanding:"(Daniel 2:21). Call upon God and rest on him, he is a sure bulwark, he will deliver you.

I'VE ANCHORED IN JESUS (L.E. JONES)

(1)   Upon life's boundless ocean where mighty billows roll,

I've fixed my hope in Jesus, blest anchor of my soul;

When trials fierce assail me as storms are gathering o'er,

I rest upon His mercy and trust him more.

Chorus:

I've anchored in Jesus, the storms of life I'll brave,

I've anchored in Jesus, I fear no wind or wave,

I've anchored in Jesus, for He hath pow'r to save,

I've anchored to the Rock of Ages.

(2)   He keeps my soul from evil and gives me blessed peace,

His voice hath stilled the waters and bid their tumults cease;

My Pilot and Deliverer, to Him I all confide,

For always when I need Him, He's at my side.

(3)   He is my Friend and Saviour, in Him my anchor's cast,

He drives away my sorrows and shields me from the blasts;

By faith I'm looking upward beyond life's troubled sea,

There I behold the haven prepared for me.

MOUNTAINS WILL MOVE
(JOHNNY HARDWICK)

(1)   I'm climbing each day up the glory land way,

The valley I've left far behind, I'm trusting the Lord

For that blessed reward, 'Tis cheering my glad heart and mind;

I'll never forget how He paid all my debt,

To purchase and set my soul free;

The mountains of doubt never more shall me rout,

And some day His face I shall see.

Chorus

The mountains will move ....when

(The mountains will move when to Him we prove,)

To Him we prove He's living in your heart and mine,

(to Him prove He's living in your heart and living in mine;)

As onward we go..His

(As onward we go His love-light will glow,)

love-light will glow, Our wonderful Saviour divine.

(love-light glow, Our wonderful Saviour, our Saviour divine.)

(2)   The mountains of sin can be cast from within

When Jesus is given control, On mountains of gloom

Sweetest flowers will bloom When we are completely made whole,

I'll never turn back from the heavenly track,

For yonder is new joy to find, I'm headed for home

And I never shall roam, Sin's valley I'm leaving behind.

(3)   So often I grieve to see men disbelieve And lightly turn Jesus away;

I wonder just how they will feel when they bow To Him on that final great day; I'd rather just wait till I enter the gate

And share all the blessings in store, For yonder His smile will be worth all the while O'er mountains I've struggled to soar.

HE IS ABLE TO DELIVER THEE

(WILLIAM A. OGDEN)

'Tis the grandest theme thru the ages rung, 'Tis the grandest theme for a

Mortal tongue; 'Tis the grandest theme that the world e'er sung__"Our God is able to deliver thee."

Chorus:

He is able to deliver thee, He is able to deliver thee;
Tho by sin opprest, Go to Him for rest: "Our God is above to deliver thee."

ABOUT THE AUTHOR

Exchange is simply a wilful act of giving out something and receiving something else in return. Not many people usually think of the likely effects of their actions and that has made them make some costly but avoidable mistakes. This book reveals some gross but avoidable mistakes of some personalities and proven solution or way out of this unhelpful habit. It is good for evangelism and counseling both young and old in righteousness.

Victoria Olubunmi Edenih has been redeemed by the blood of the Lamb. Her passion is to daily live for the Lord in holiness and righteousness and to daily lift the Saviour for the world to see in everything she does and make heaven at last. She is married to Francis Oviomaigho Edenih. They are blessed with a gift.

www.ingramcontent.com/pod-product-compliance
Lightning Source LLC
Chambersburg PA
CBHW072038060426
42449CB00010BA/2327